Sisters Are
Forever Friends

a very
special book
created especially
for sisters

Ashley Rice

Blue Mountain Press ™

Boulder, Colorado

Friends may come and go,
but a sister remains
in your heart
and in your life forever.

You're My Amazing Sister, and I Love You

Though I might not always say it
with exactly the right words
(or even out loud),
I want you to know
it makes me feel good
and very proud
to have a sister like you.

You know where I come from
because you come from there, too.

And no matter what happens
in this world,
I will always be there for you.
You've been my friend
right from the start.

You've got a unique place
in my life, days, and heart.
Even if we fuss or fight,
I know it will be all right.

Where I come from, you do, too.
You're my amazing sister,
and I love you.

Why I Love You, Sister

- You're there for me.

- You are unique.

- You know where I'm coming from.

- We've laughed a lot together and cried some.

- We get through our differences, and together we shine.

- No one else could ever replace you in my life.

- You are a beautiful person.

- You make me smile.

- You make me forget my troubles for a while.

- You make me think.

- You make me grin.

- You give me everything you've got
  when it comes to being a sister.

You ARe Special to Me in a Way No One Else Is

You always caRe
about what happens in my day —
no matteR how big oR how small.
You listen like no one else does.
And when I lose my diRection,
you aRe always theRe
to guide me back home safely.
I know that you see
the best in me,
but you aRe honest with me too
and help me to see
what is going on in my life.
I'd tRust you with anything,
and I know that you
would neveR betRay that tRust.
You know me so well,
and I know you so well,
that ouR heaRts will always
be inteRconnected.

I love having you around
to hang out with and
to brighten my days.
I love that you are never afraid
to be yourself.
You teach me things
that no one else could
ever teach me
and tell me things that I hold
dearly in my heart.
There is no one else like you
in the world
and no one else who can
make me see things
the way you do.
You're my friend for life.

You're Incredible!

There are sisters who are trustworthy.
There are sisters who are true.
There are sisters who will go
as far as they can
to help you.
There are sisters who are
daring and kind.
There are sisters who are strong.
There are sisters who are extraordinary.
And you, my sister, are all of
these things...
and more.

You're always there for me,
especially when other people are gone.
You make me laugh at everything —
whether I'm feeling good or feeling blue —
and even when something goes wrong.
You remind me of who I am inside
and you make me feel like I belong to
something pretty great
(which is true).

I feel lucky to have a sister like you.

You Inspire Me to Be
a Better Person

It is so fun to chat with you
about what goes on in our lives,
and I don't know what I would do
without you to show me the way.
You surprise me with
the different things you do
to make life better for others.
We have so much in common
that I sometimes feel like we're twins —
but there are enough differences
between us that we constantly challenge
and push each other to try new things.
There is so much that I wouldn't
have done if it weren't for you;
there were so many times when
I would have struggled
if it weren't for having you
by my side to help me out.
You make every day a gift,
and you inspire me to be
a better person.

In my life, I've known
some amazing people
who've forever changed me.
I don't know if they realize
how much they helped me
when I felt discouraged, uncertain,
or simply blue.
It could have been their grins,
their words, their examples,
or their real kindness
that pulled me through.
How much I appreciate them,
I'm not sure they will ever understand...
but you should know,
one of those amazing people
is you.

Growing Up with You
Is One of the Best
Experiences I Have Ever Had

You've been there for me
through every triumph and every tear —
cheering me on and cheering me up.
You remember the times
we spent together when we were little.
We share memories of
scraped knees, boys, school,
work, and friends.
We will always be together
because we have the common
bond of family and the past
to keep us going
through the hardest of times.
I will always remember you as you were,
but I embrace who you have
become and continue to become,
as you grow more beautiful
and confident and strong
with each passing day.

CONGRATS!

I am so lucky to
have you in my life
and to have had you there
all along —
seeing me through my days
with smiles and laughter
and lots of love.
You are the best sister
anyone could ever
wish for.

I Am Home When
I Am with You

Home is more than a place
with four square walls,
windows, and a front door.
Home is a place where
we are surrounded by people
who care about our welfare —
where we always feel
loved and accepted.
Home is a place where
we can retreat,
reassess,
lick our wounds,
and get out there again.
Home is a place where we can go
when we feel like
the world is against us
and nothing is going our way.

When we arrive at home,
suddenly everything
looks better and brighter.
Home is a place of understanding
and the hope of a more
wonderful tomorrow.
And I know that I am home
when I am with you.

Our Differences
Make Us
Shine Brightly

We may be different,
but your strength guides me
throughout my life.
We may have different favorite colors,
jobs, and paths,
but you give me courage,
and it's fun to laugh with you
about what happens during our days.
We share life's experiences
with each other,
teach each other,
and walk together
into the future.
If I could choose a sister —
anyone in all the world —
I would pick you.

I love how I can be
myself around you
and you will never judge me.
I can be silly,
and you will be silly with me.
I can go through hard times and cry,
and you will be there.
I love how you can be
yourself around me,
with no reservations
and no holding back,
just as you are.
I love that I can talk with you
about anything
and you will gently understand.
I love that we can be
together through all
kinds of weather,
always being ourselves —
the true sisters we are.

Sisters Are...

Sisters are awesome and unique and incredible.

Sisters are angels and confidantes and friends.

Sisters are outrageous and fun and comforting.

Sisters are rare and treasured and appreciated.

Sisters are radiant and star-like and wonderful.

Sisters are listeners and tellers and speakers.

Sisters are finders of the unexpected
and seekers and companions.

Sisters are knowing and
unforgettable and one of a kind.

Sisters are special...
for the gifts they share that
come straight from the heart.

Sisters Are the Heart and Soul of Life

Sisters are there
through thick and thin.
They pick up the pieces
whenever anything goes wrong.
They hold our hands
through the scary parts
and listen to our troubles.
They know everything about us
and like us anyway.
They cheer us on
when things are going great,
and they are a shoulder
to cry on when things
aren't as good as they could be.
We would be nowhere in life
without our sisters.
They are around to guide us,
encourage us, and make us smile.

Sisters are family and friendship.
They are sunny days
and comfort in the storms of life.
Sisters are there
to understand and not judge,
to accept, and to nourish.
Sisters are friends when others
have gone away;
they are smiles that keep us
going throughout the days.
Sisters keep our secrets
and give us confidence
when we need it.
Sisters are dear to our hearts
and essential to our lives.

23

Where Would I Be Without You?

I never would have gotten as far
as I have without you –
never would have smiled so much,
never would have laughed so much,
never would have tried so much,
or fallen down then stood up tall so much.

I never would have gotten this far
at all without you,
never would have seen the same grand things,
never would have dreamed the same big dreams.

You make me feel like
the world has endless possibilities.
You make me feel comforted
during life's rainstorms.
You give me hope,
like sunshine breaking
through the clouds.

You make me feel like
anything is possible... anything.

You've Got What It Takes to Succeed

Sometimes life can be hard!
Sometimes there don't seem to be
any answers —
not even the stars seem to know
which way to go.
But you've got
the answers inside you.
You've got what you need
to pull you through
and to face the road in front of you,
wherever it goes.

You've got courage
and bravery.
You've got spunk,
and you've got smiles
in your back pocket
to help you through
difficult days.
No matter what happens,
you've got what it takes
to succeed.

I Admire You
So Much

- When you know what has to be done...
    you do it.

- When you have a plan...
    you see it through.

- When you've got a dream in mind...
    you pursue it.

- You don't let what others say
    discourage or overencourage you.

- When there's grunt work to be done...
    you get through it.

● You are aware of the bigger picture
   and the small ones, too.

● You stand up tall again and go on
   Right after you temporarily blow it
   (a true sign of courage).

And these are just a few Reasons why
   I constantly admire you.

Keep Being You

No one could ever copy you —
you're a unique
and completely amazing individual.
You're filled with sunshine,
and every day
you make a difference
with what you do.

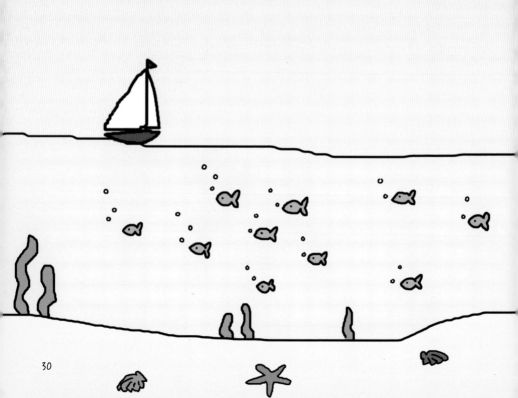

You are a star,
constant and true.
Your smile, your hopes,
light up a room.

So whether today
you win or lose...
forget past pains and
keep being you!

No One Could Ever Take Your Place

You are irreplaceable.
There's no one else
who can hold my hand
in the exact same way,
no one else who is so good
at making my tears go away.
You give the best advice,
listen the hardest
to my hopes and fears,
and grow with me
throughout the years.

You are incredible and real
and very special.
You stand by your friends
and family
and are the best at keeping secrets.
I hope that nothing
ever comes between us
and that we will always be
as close as ever.
I know this will come true,
just as I know that you
will continue to be
the exceptional person that you are —
someone who I am very
happy to have as my sister.

You Were Meant for Greatness

As you greet each new day,
know that great things
lie ahead for you.
Keep sunshine
in your pocket
for the times
when you will need it.
Keep a fire in your heart
and put your best foot forward
on the path that lies ahead,
because these will be
some of the best days
that you have ever had.

Know that all the stars
in the sky are watching over you
to keep the sacred sparkle
in your life and in your step.
Know that each day keeps you safe
and that there is something out there
bigger than you are
that keeps you in tune
with the universe
and with every little thing that's
going on in the world.
Know that everything will be okay
today and tomorrow.
Know that you are treasured
for the unique

and strong and sparkly
individual person that you are...
every day of your life.

Leaves fall,
things change,
but sisters' hearts
stay strong
as we move on.

For as many different days
as there are in the sun,
as many different races
that we've lost
or we've won...

...and into all life's
changes through which —
like thoroughbreds —
we run...

Leaves fall,
things change,
and sisters' hearts
stay strong.

A Sister Is...

A sister is someone you can
count on.
A sister is someone who sees
the best in you.
A sister is someone who has seen you
at your worst but somehow
is still there for you.
A sister is someone who has
been there from the start.
A sister is someone who
remains in your heart.

A sister is a confidante.
A sister is there when no one else
    could understand.
A sister is a miracle.
A sister is a dream come true.
A sister is a friend forever.
A sister is a very special
    person in your life.

I Can Talk with You About Anything

Some people
spend their whole lives
feeling blue
because they never
find someone real
and forgiving and honest
that they can talk to
about all the joys
and sorrows
and funny instances
that go on in their lives.

Some people
go through
their whole lives
without a clue about
what it means
to be okay
with who they are
because they are without
the bright and shining star
of (real) friendship
in their lives.
(That's why I feel so lucky
to have a friend
and a sister like you.)

You're the Very Definition of a Good Friend

Good friends are not the people
who will like you only for
the brand of jeans you are wearing
or your new, stylish purse.
They are not the people
who support you only
when you're winning.
A good friend will be there
whether you're up or down,
whether you're having a good day
or a terrible one.

And being a good friend
means doing the same thing —
sticking around for the
good times and bad.
Thanks for being a good friend!

Thanks for Always Being There

Thanks for forgiving me
whenever I make the wrong choice.
You never hold it against me,
but instead you
help me to stand strong again.
You are a comfort in the storm,
a ray of sunshine on bad days,
and a chocolate sundae treat
when I need it the most.
Sometimes, you know me
better than I know myself.

Because you are there for me,
I am stronger, wiser, and kinder.
Because you are by my side,
I am able to face anything that
is in my path.
You cheer me up when I am down,
and you always seem to know
the right thing to say
when things aren't going my way.
Without you, I would not be
the person I am today.
Thanks for always being there for me
and for seeing the good in me
even when I can't.
You are the best sister ever.

I'll Always Be There for You, Too!

If you've got secrets you want to tell,
we can talk all day long.
If your dreams get broken somehow,
I'll remind you that you belong.
If you need someplace to hide,
you can hold my hand for a while.
If your sky begins to fall,
I'll stay with you till you smile.
Whenever you need some space,
there's my room — you can take it.
If someone breaks your heart,
together we'll unbreak it.

When you feel sad or empty inside,
I'll show you you're not alone.
If you get lost out there,
I'll come and take you home.
I'll go with you somewhere else
when you need to get away.
And when nothing seems to be going right
and you need a friend...
I'll stay.

Even When We're Not Together...

I hold a place for you in my heart —
just like I'd save a seat for you
right next to me at the movies,
a restaurant, on a bench in a tree-lined park,
or any other place in life I know
how to get to.
Having a sister like you
is an incredible thing.
It feels good to know
that we come from the same branch
of the very same tree.

Even when we can't
be together,
Remember the strong bond
that ties us together.
Though the miles
may be long,
you're always right here,
in my heart.

Don't Ever Forget This

You are a very
special person
with many gifts
and many dreams.
You are a very
special person
with a very
special heart
and a very special
way of being yourself.